Mad Margaret Experiments
with the
Scientific Method

by
Eric Braun

illustrated by
Robin Boyden

PICTURE WINDOW BOOKS
a capstone imprint

Thanks to our advisers for their expertise, research, and advice:
Dr. Paul Ohmann, Associate Professor of Physics, University of St. Thomas
Terry Flaherty, PhD, Professor of English, Minnesota State University, Mankato

Editor: Shelly Lyons
Designer: Lori Bye
Art Director: Nathan Gassman
Production Specialist: Danielle Ceminsky
The illustrations in this book were created digitally.

Picture Window Books
1710 Roe Crest Drive
North Mankato, MN 56003
www.capstonepub.com

Library of Congress Cataloging-in-Publication Data
Braun, Eric, 1971-
  Mad Margaret experiments with the scientific method / by Eric Braun ;
illustrations by Robin Boyden.
      p. cm. — (Capstone Picture Window Books. In the science lab)
  Includes index.
ISBN 978-1-4048-7373-5 (library binding)
ISBN 978-1-4048-7710-8 (paperback)
ISBN 978-1-4048-7986-7 (ebook PDF)
1. Science—Methodology—Juvenile literature. 2. Science—
Experiments—Juvenile literature. I. Boyden, Robin, 1983- ill. II. Title.

Q175.2.B73 2013
507.8—dc23

                                    2012001010

Printed in the United States of America in Stevens Point, Wisconsin.
                  072013   007605R

I'M MAD MARGARET, BUT I'M NOT REALLY MAD. MY FRIENDS JUST LIKE TO CALL ME A MAD SCIENTIST, BECAUSE I'M CRAZY ABOUT SCIENCE.

I have lots of good ideas. People usually come to me when they need help with a problem. I don't know everything. I just know how to figure things out using the scientific method.

"I've been sneezing," Jasper said.

"A sneezing problem?" I asked.

4

"Yes, but I sneeze only at my friend Donna's house."

"Ah," I said. "The Case of the Mysterious Sneezes."

"What do we do?" asked Jasper.

I TOLD JASPER WE COULD USE THE SCIENTIFIC METHOD. THE SCIENTIFIC METHOD IS A SERIES OF STEPS. THE STEPS HELP US FIGURE OUT A PROBLEM. THE FIRST STEP IS TO ASK A QUESTION.

"OUR QUESTION IS: WHY DOES JASPER SNEEZE AT DONNA'S HOUSE?" I SAID.

"That's a good question," Jasper said.

"Indeed."

"Well, what's the next step?" asked Jasper.

I grabbed my notebook and pencil.
"The next step is to gather information.
Tell me what you do at Donna's house," I said.

"OH, IT'S THE BEST. WE PLAY IN THE BACKYARD,"
Jasper answered.

"WE MAKE MUD ROADS, BIG CASTLES OUT OF ROCKS,
AND MOATS WITH WATER."

The Scientific Method

Step One:
Ask a question.

Step Two:
Gather information.

"That sounds really fun!"

"You can play with us," Jasper said.

"Thanks," I answered, "but first I want to figure out why you're sneezing at Donna's house."

"DO YOU SNEEZE WHEN YOU'RE OUT IN THE YARD?" I ASKED.

JASPER THOUGHT FOR A MINUTE WHILE HE TOOK OFF HIS HELMET.
"NO, ONLY IN THE HOUSE."

"GREAT!" I SAID.

"WHY IS THAT SO GREAT?" JASPER ASKED.

"IT GIVES US MORE INFORMATION. LET ME ASK YOU THIS:
WHAT DO YOU DO INSIDE?"

JASPER KNOCKED ON THE DOOR TO DONNA'S HOUSE. "I'LL SHOW YOU," HE SAID.

Donna answered the door and invited us in.

"Donna, this is Margaret," said Jasper.

"Nice to meet you," said Donna. "This is Ringo," she said, rubbing her face in the cat's fur.

"Hi, Ringo," I said. I turned to Jasper and continued, "So what do you two do when you play inside?"

"Well, mostly we—AH-CHOO!" Jasper sniffled. "Mostly we listen to loud music and pretend to play guitar." He sneezed again.

Step One:
Ask a question.

Step Two:
Gather information.

Step Three:
Form a hypothesis.

"Hmm," I said, making a note in my notepad. "Donna, does your family always keep the windows wide open? It's drafty in here."

"Most of the time," said Donna.

"Then we have enough information to go on to the next step: Form a hypothesis," I said. "That's a guess about what we think might be the answer to our question. In this case, the hypothesis is a guess about what makes Jasper sneeze at Donna's house."

13

"Do you have a guess about what's making Jasper sneeze?" asked Donna.

"Well, since he never sneezes outside, we can rule out mud and rock castles," I answered.

"Whew, I'm glad," said Jasper. He sneezed, and Donna handed him a tissue.

"And since he's sneezing now, even with the music off, I don't think he's sneezing because of the loud music," I said.

The Scientific Method

Step One:
Ask a question.

Step Two:
Gather information.

Step Three:
Form a hypothesis.

Step Four:
Test the hypothesis.

"I bet he's sneezing because of the drafty windows," suggested Donna.

"Good hypothesis," I said. "The next step is to do an experiment to test the hypothesis. Let's close all the windows."

15

We closed all the windows in the house, then sat on the couch and waited. Donna put on a song, loud, and we pretended to play. At first Jasper didn't even sniffle. "This might be it!" Donna shouted.

"**Aaaaaah-choooooo!**" Jasper replied.

"Guess not," Donna said. She turned off the music. "What do we do when an experiment shows that the hypothesis is wrong?"

16

"We look at our information again. Then we form a new hypothesis," I answered. "Is there any place in the house where the cats never go?"

"My brother's room," said Donna. "He doesn't like cats."

"Perfect," I said. "My hypothesis is that the cats are making Jasper sneeze. I think he's allergic to cats. Donna, please lead us to your brother's room."

17

"Try not to bother him," said Donna.

The three of us sat and waited. And waited.
And waited.

Jasper did not sneeze. "Yes!" he hollered.

"Shhh," said Donna, pointing at her brother.

"It seems like our hypothesis
is right," I said. "But
we should run another
experiment to be sure."

18

So we climbed up into Donna's attic, where no cats ever went. Jasper did not sneeze there either.

"Now I know that the cats make me sneeze," Jasper said. "I'm happy to know the answer, but I'm sad I can't play here anymore."

"We'll just have to play outside more," Donna said. "Come on."

The three of us played in the backyard. It was a blast.

"Oh, I almost forgot," I said. "The last step of the scientific method is to share the results. Jasper, you should tell your parents. Maybe a doctor can help you with the sneezing."

"Cool," Jasper said. "Thanks for your help with the scientific method. Next time I have a problem, maybe I can solve it myself."

"Of course you can," I said. "But it might be more fun if I could help you."

"Definitely," said Donna and Jasper.

"Well, it looks like the Case of the Mysterious Sneezes is officially closed!"

The Scientific Method

Step One:
Ask a question.

Step Two:
Gather information.

Step Three:
Form a hypothesis.

Step Four:
Test the hypothesis.

Step Five:
Share the results.

GLOSSARY

allergic—when something, like a bee sting or pollen in the air, makes someone feel sick; many allergies make you sneeze

experiment—a scientific test to find out how something works

hypothesis—an idea about how or why something happens; you can test your idea to see if it is right

result—the outcome of something

scientific method—a step-by-step process that scientists use to solve problems

scientist—a person who studies the world around us

TO LEARN MORE

More Books to Read

Benbow, Ann, and Colin Mably. *Master the Scientific Method with Fun Life Science Projects*. Real Life Science Experiments. Berkeley Heights, N.J.: Enslow Publishers, 2010.

Glass, Susan. *Analyze This!: Understanding the Scientific Method*. How to Be a Scientist. Chicago: Heineman Library, 2007.

Taylor-Butler, Christine. *Experiments with Liquids*. My Science Investigations. Chicago: Heinemann Library, 2012.

Internet Sites

FactHound offers a safe, fun way to find Internet sites related to this book. All of the sites on FactHound have been researched by our staff.

Here's all you do:

Visit *www.facthound.com*

Type in this code: 9781404873735

Super-cool stuff!

Check out projects, games and lots more at www.capstonekids.com

INDEX

LOOK FOR ALL THE BOOKS IN THE SERIES:

CAPTAIN KIDD'S CREW EXPERIMENTS WITH
SINKING AND FLOATING

DO-4U THE ROBOT EXPERIENCES
FORCES AND MOTION

Gertrude and Reginald the Monsters Talk about
LIVING AND NONLIVING

JOE-JOE THE WIZARD BREWS UP
SOLIDS, LIQUIDS, AND GASES

LANCE DRAGON DEFENDS HIS CASTLE WITH
SIMPLE MACHINES

MAD MARGARET EXPERIMENTS WITH THE
SCIENTIFIC METHOD